Victorious Living

How To Live a Victorious Life

By

Cammie B. Jeffress

ISBN: 1-4107-1948-0 (e-book)
ISBN: 1-4107-1949-9 (Paperback)

This book is printed on acid free paper.

All scripture quotations, unless otherwise
indicated, are taken from the Holy Bible.
The author has inserted italics and bolding
used in quotations from scripture.

1stBooks – rev. 6/13/03

Dedicated to

my family with love.

Che M. Brown, Kwame R. Brown, and

Kimberly L. Cobb

In memory of

George and Camilla Jane Randall

Overseer Harriette E. Wood
Founder, St. Paul Pentecostal Church,
Incorporated, 1972

Deaconess Euphranize R. Golden

Acknowledgements

I thank God for the efforts, encourag-ement, and compasssion to the many people who have contributed to this book. I especially want to thank

> M. Kaye Brown
> Sharon Harriston Henery, Pencil Pal
> Lawanda Randall

for their editorial expertise.

TABLE OF CONTENTS

INTRODUCTION

Praise the Lord. There are so many Christians today who are living defeated lives. This should not be. Jesus Christ has gained the keys to death, Hell, and the grave. We can overcome because of Him.

God is pouring out His Holy Spirit onto his people. It is time for God's people to use the power that He has given. *"But ye shall receive power, after that the Holy Ghost is come upon you..." (Acts 1:8).* We are victorious in every walk of life. We are not defeated in any area. The death of Jesus Christ, on the cross, signified victory. He overcame all: sicknesses, diseases, situations, and circumstances. He was obedient to God, and through obedience to Christ today, we can be victorious in the work He has called us to do.

The purpose of this book is to reach as many souls as possible in the spreading of God's Word. The objective is to make the Word so clear that even a child would be able to understand.

There are millions of people today who are lost in this world of sin. Some are looking to find ways to escape. Some are confused and physically drained in their search for answers. I, too, was that way until one day I found Jesus Christ. The puzzle piece missing from my life was found. I learned that Jesus was the answer. When I couldn't find my way, didn't know which way to turn or where to go, Jesus was always there for me. I learned to look to the Lord and praise Him for all things big or small, good or bad. Out of all the evil, God helped me to find the good.

We should be able to give thanks to God for all things. I didn't know how to praise Him, but He taught me. Therefore, I want to teach others. If you are willing, you can learn. I learned through situations to praise the Lord, for the JOY of the Lord is our strength. God is our refuge, our present help in the time of trouble.

For so long, many of God's people have allowed the adversary to stop them from praising God. I want to convey to the people the power of praise and deliverance. In praising God, deliverance comes. Through singing hymns and spiritual songs and making melody to God, the adversary must flee. But, most of all, the adversary flees when the Word of God is spoken.

It is time-out for weak saints. It is time for children of God to be strong and learn how to grow in the admonition of the Lord. In reading this book, I pray you will come to know the importance of praising God, in order to be delivered and to develop the ability to recognize the adversary.

God intends for His people to be delivered from every obstacle. To go forth in true praise, you as Christians must be delivered. You are unable to give the highest praise to our Lord and Saviour Jesus Christ, if you are bound. You must be free in the spirit.

Over the course of my life, Jesus Christ, through His Holy Spirit, taught me how to be victorious; how to be positive; how to be firm and strong; and how to lean and trust in Him only. He is always there for me, just as He will always be there for you.

I pray you will enjoy the richness of information provided, that your inward man will be fed with the riches of life. Keep in mind that this book covers specific areas that I find are the hardest for Christians. I can only give you what God has given unto me. Once you read this book, you will be able to surpass any dark cloud.

x

Importance of Worship

"The hand of the Lord was upon him..."

2 Kings 3:14-15

CHAPTER 1

Music enhances the anointing. We need to understand the role music plays in affecting the prophet's ministry. In 2 Kings 3:15-16, ***"And now bring me a minstrel. And it came to pass, when the minstrel played, that the hand of the Lord came upon him"***. Elisha called for a minstrel, and his anointing was enhanced. Here we see that Elisha went on to give the message of victory that God gave him. "The hand of the Lord was upon him." That hand represents the **anointing**.

Music comes under the ministry of helps. (1 Corinthians 12:28). For it is necessary to help the Preachers and Prophets to come forth with power. The music of ministry is discussed in 1

Corinthians 14:15 ***"I will sing with the spirit, and I will sing with the understanding also."*** It is one of the greatest helps. Many individuals can sing; but, all are not anointed by God.

Music plays a great role in the worship service. It sets the pace for the service and it helps in worshiping God. The musician's role is significant. If the right kind of music is played, it breaks the yokes. It affects all of the ministries. The preacher can preach with power, the exalter can sing with greater power, and the anointing will flow in all the offices. Music can help ministers—not just prophets—because all ministers must minister under the anointing and the singers must sing with the anointing.

Those who stand in the prophetic role will be able to benefit more from the music because the prophet must be more sensitive to the spirit. It is very important that the musicians pray before playing. It is very important that the exalters pray before coming forth to sing in the worship service.

You cannot come into the Church of God after a long day at work and expect to stand and sing praises before the Lord. You must empty yourself from all cares, knowing that God is Jehovah-Jireh, your provider; Jehovah-Nissi, lift your banner high; Jehovah Shalom, your prince of peace; and El Elyon; the most high God. He is a God of more than enough. At this point you have ceased from all cares and laughing and are serious.

It is a great responsibility that has been given to those who are anointed to sing and play musical instruments. They are responsible for souls whether they accept it or reject it. God is going to hold them responsible. There will be times in your life when you might be down, sick in your body, and tired in your spirit. Nevertheless, you must elevate your mind higher to the Lord. Your main concern is the people and all emphasis must not be placed on self. Paul said, "*...I crucify self daily.*" Yes, the Lord has set a great task on those who are called in the Ministry of Music, and it is not to be taken lightly.

The Right Song

Musicians and singers must be in tune with the spirit as much as the ministers. There are times when the pastors, ministers, and prophets need help. The spirit of the people will get low and the right song, at the right time, can set the pace for these ministries to go forth. That is why Elisha needed a little help. He said, ***"Bring me minstrel..." (2 Kings 3:15).***

The Spirit in the church might start out on a low key. Someone comes along and sings a song and the Spirit begins to flow. Someone else comes along and sings a low-key song causing the person whom the Lord has used to break the yoke to interrupt the Spirit. It is important that you know the moving of the Holy Spirit. Ask the Lord to give you what to sing and direct you when to sing. For example, the song "I've Got Peace Like a River" is being sung, the anointing is flowing, the individuals are praising God, and the souls of the people have been lifted. Then someone comes behind that individual and sings "The Lord Will Make a Way," and the whole purpose is defeated because the individual has caused the tone of the service to drop.

Know the Holy Spirit. Know the moving of the Holy Spirit. God wants us to be aware of Him. Take time to listen to what the Holy Spirit is saying. Sing the song so the Lord might get the glory. We are not to sing or play musical instruments for our own glory, but for the GLORY OF THE LORD. We are nothing without God. We cannot do anything without Him.

Garments of Praise

"Put on the garments of praise for the spirit of heaviness..."

Isaiah 61:3

CHAPTER 2

Most Churches have a space of **devotional** time before starting the regular worship service. What is the purpose of this time? It is used to bring us into the presence of God, and we do this by singing directly unto Him. It also allows us space to give a spiritual testimony: telling what the Lord has done in our lives. ***"Give thanks unto the Lord; call upon his name: make known his deeds among the people" (Psalms 105:1)***. Some branches of Zion do not start with this type of service; therefore, you must enter into His gates with thanksgiving and into His courts with praise in your hearts. Yes, it is time for us to understand the importance of devotions.

A **Devotional Service** consists of one or two people who are called **Devotional Leaders** because they lead the church into devotions. Variations of songs come naturally to them and they must be in right fellowship with the Lord. Everyone is not a Devotional Leader or Praiser. Through their singing the captives are set free, and yokes are destroyed. They must know the moving of the Spirit. They must know what songs to sing, when to exhort the service, and when to end the service. The Holy Spirit is their guide. They must be able to hear the voice of the Lord. Every song is not giving praise to God, and every testimony is not giving praise to God. They **must** know the difference.

Wherever you are, *"...Enter into His gates with thanksgiving and into His court with praise..." (Psalms 100:4).* Give God the thanks for everything. *"In every thing give thanks: for this is the will of God in Christ Jesus concerning you" (1 Thessalonians 5:18).* If the Lord had not been on your side, and brought you out of darkness into the marvelous light, where would you be? Therefore, you have a right to praise the Lord. Let the redeemed of the Lord say so. So let's

"Rejoice in the Lord alway: and again I say, Rejoice" (Philippians 4:4). All your cares, anxieties, and stress will be relieved once you learn how to praise the Lord.

When you come into God's presence be mindful that you are on **HOLY GROUND.** Wherever you are, He is. Our lives must be in fellowship with Christ, whether you are leading a devotional service or seated in the congregation. You must be in right standing with God in order to enter into His presence. We must praise Him with our whole heart. **"I will praise thee with my whole heart: before the gods will I sing praise unto thee" (Psalms 138:1)**.

How to Come Forth in Praise

First, we **praise** God with gladness. We must ask the Lord to cleanse us from all unrighteousness. Leave our burdens, circumstances, difficulties, and sicknesses outside as we enter into His presence. There should be some excitement in you when you enter into the House of the Lord. David said **"I was glad when they said unto me; Let us go into the house of the Lord" (Psalms 123:1)**. There is peace, joy, healing, and rest for your weary souls. **"Come unto me, all ye that**

7

labour and are heavy laden, and I will give you rest" (Matthew 11:28).

Second, we **serve** the Lord in Spirit and in Truth. **"Let the words of Christ dwell in you richly...in psalms and hymns and spiritual songs, singing with grace in your hearts to the Lord" (Colossians 3:16).** Be honest and be truthful in your communication with the Lord. Let the Holy Spirit lead you in what to say and in what to sing. Render praises unto the Lord with a clean heart. Before you begin to praise Him, ask Him to forgive you for all your sins: sins of omission and commission. For He does not hear you when there is iniquity in your hearts. **"For thy name's sake, O Lord, pardon mine iniquity; for it is great" (Psalms 25:11).** Remember, only the pure in heart shall see God.

Third, serve Him with joy. The joy of the Lord is our strength. **"Then he said...for the joy of the Lord is your strength" (Nehemiah 8:10)**. We draw water from the well of salvation. **"Therefore with joy shall ye draw water out of the wells of salvation" (Isaiah 12:3)**. Make a joyful noise unto the Lord. Praise Him, with instruments, tambourines, and with a dance. **"Let them praise his name in the dance; let them sing praises unto him with the timbrel and harp" (Psalms**

149:3) *"Let everything that hath breath, Praise ye the Lord" (Psalms 150:6)*

Sometimes, you might have to leap for joy. When Moses brought the children of Israel out of Egypt and they crossed the Red Sea safely, Miriam began to praise God with her tambourine and to dance. After David brought the ark of God from Obededom's house to Jerusalem, he was so overjoyed that he began leaping for joy until his apparel fell off. ***"And David danced before the Lord with all his might...And as the ark of the Lord came into the city of David, Michael Saul's daughter looked...and saw King David leaping and dancing before the Lord..." (2 Samuel 6:12-16).*** As we come into the House of the Lord, we too, should be rejoicing with gladness that we made it through another day in this sin-sick world.

Fourth, we praise Him in **trials and tribulations**. In the midst of adversities, let nothing separate you from praising God. (Romans 8:35) Although the storms of life may blow and trials and tribulations may come, praise God. Be persistent in your walk with Him. Be mindful of who He is.

Press through all the obstacles that are in your way. Look, believe, and receive from the Lord all that He has for you.

In my earlier years as a Born-Again Christian, I had to learn to sing and worship the Lord in spite of all circumstances. I used to come to the House of God with my head down, feeling down trodden. Someone would begin singing a song and all of a sudden, I had forgotten about my state and remembered who Jesus was, what He had done for me, and most of all, who I was. I realized that I was victorious and not defeated as the enemy wanted me to believe. The Holy Spirit brought to my remembrance God's Word, **"Lift up your head, O ye gates;...ye everlasting doors; and the King of glory shall come in..." (Psalms 24:9).** Let Him in, for He is the Lord of Lords, and Kings of Kings. Let Him in.

Foundation of Music

"Jubal was the first musician inventor of the harp and flute."

(Genesis 4:17-21)

CHAPTER 3

Let us take a look at the foundation of music. Music, as defined by Webster's Dictionary, is the art of ordering tones or sounds in succession, in combination, and in temporal relationships to produce a composition having unity and continuity. These sounds are done by vocally or instrumentally, and have rhythm, melody, or harmony. There are three basic components of the Music Ministry: singing, playing musical instruments, and directing a choir or singers.

How did music come into existence? Cain had a son, Enoch. Enoch had a son, Irad. Enoch's great great grandson was

Lamech. Lamech had two sons, Jabal and Jubal. Jubal was the first musician inventor of the harp and flute. (Genesis 4:17-21)

We are now going to take a look at scriptural foundations, which explain the three components. They are **Singers, Musicians, and Choirs.** God told King David that He had blessed the house of Obededom, and that He wanted him to bring the ark of God from the house of Obededom to the city of Jerusalem (2 Samuel 6:12). David prepared a place for the ark, organized the Temple worship, and ordered the Levite leaders to organize singers into an orchestra, to play music with psalteries, harps, and cymbals. *"...brethren to be the singers with instruments of musick, psalteries and harps and cymbals, sounding, by lifting up the voice with joy" (1 Chronicles 15:16)*. The Levities were to oversee the work of the Temple. They set apart the sons of Asaph, Heman and Jeduthun for the ministry of music in the Temple. *"...service of the sons of Asaph, and of Heman, and of Jeduthun, who should prophesy with harps, with psalteries, and with cymbals..." (Chronicles 25:1).*

Singers

Asaph's sons were **Singers**. Asaph himself was a Choir Director of the Singers. Asaph was to lead them to sing joyful songs accompanied by musical instruments, lyres, harps (guitar) and cymbals (plates of brass) (1 Chronicles 15:16; 16:1 & 6; Nehemiah 12:46).

Musicians

Jeduthun's sons were Musicians. Jeduthun was placed in charge of music in the house of the Lord (1 Chronicle 16:42; 25:6). As he led in giving thanks and praises to God, he was accompanied by musical instruments, which were used to make melody unto the Lord. You will find that most churches have pianos, organs, drums, guitars, flutes, trumpets, and saxophones.

Musicians and Singers

Heman's sons were Musicians and Singers. They ministered before the tabernacle with singing and instruments. Heman was a choir director; he had 14 sons and 3 daughters who were used as musicians and chorus singers. His family was musically inclined.

Asaph, Jeduthun, and Heman and their families were trained in singing praises to the Lord, and were gifted with the ability to play instruments.

Significance of Music

Music draws others when the songs have a meaning. Songs should be geared to non-Christians encouraging them to have faith in God. Christian music **must** minister to others. It is important that we sing with the spirit and with understanding also. We should sing praises daily. ***"For God is the King of all the earth: sing ye praises with understanding" (Psalms 47:7)***. Do not just sing to sing, but understand the meaning of the song. God can minister to your spirit through songs of comfort and encouragement. Always speak to yourself in psalms and hymns.

There is a wide variety of talents in all of us. Everyone is not gifted in the music field, but is gifted in other areas. It is not enough to be able to sing and play instruments, but it is important to be under the anointing of God.

"O Sing unto the Lord a new song; sing unto the Lord, all the earth"

(Psalms 96:1). Those who operate in these gifts and talents are to go forward as never before. Continue to be steadfast in your praises. Come forth and sing of the mercies of God. Praise the name of God in song and thanksgiving. Glorify God for his mercy. Praise the Lord with the sound of the trumpet, psaltery, harps, timbrel (refers to drums, tambourines) stringed instruments, flutes, and loud cymbals.

Preparation—God's House

Take time to pray and confess your sins before coming to the house of God. **(Amos 5:21-23)** Here we find God was angry at the Israelites because they were professing His name with their lips while denying Him in their hearts. We **must** remember that **sin** and **service do not mix**. Therefore, the Word of God says in 1 John 1:9, *"If we confess our sins, he is faithful and just to forgive us our sins, and to cleanse us from all unrighteousness".*

Whatever goes wrong before you enter into His tabernacle, leave it on the outside and let go. Come into the presence of God knowing that He is your burden bearer.

Spirit of Liberty

"If the Son therefore shall make you free, ye shall be free indeed."

John 8:36

CHAPTER 4

It is time for God's people to be able to praise Him in all situations with a free spirit. ***"Stand fast therefore in the liberty wherewith Christ hath made us free, and be not entangled again with the yoke of bondage" (Galatians 5:1)***. Jesus died for us **all** to be **free**. He arose from the grave, went down into the uttermost parts of the earth, and took the keys of Hell and death, setting the captives free. The adversary wants to bind you, but you can be free. We are overcomers because Jesus overcame. Let us discuss some of the keys to freedom. ***"And I will*** *give the keys of the kingdom of heaven" (Matthew 16:19)*.

PEACE

Christians have problems in this area because their minds are constantly under attack. Learn to keep your mind on **Jesus**. *"...the peace of God which passeth all understanding..." (Philippians 4:7).* Be anxious for nothing. God will give you the strength in the mist of confusion. For He is not the author of confusion. *"For God is not the author of confusion, but of peace" (1 Corinthians 14:33)*.

We need to turn unto God from the error of our ways. If God's people turn they will have peace. Pray for peace because in God there is security. **Jesus** told His disciples *"Let not your heart be troubled..." (John 14:1)*. He gave us His peace; He left it here on the record for us. *"Peace I leave with you, my peace I give unto you; not as the world giveth, give I unto you..." (John 14:27)* So many times we let everything rule us, and our lives. But Paul said to the Church of Colosse *"...let the peace of God rule in your hearts..." (Colossians 3:15)*.

The adversary comes to kill, steal, and destroy. Don't let him steal your peace. He toys with your mind by bringing you the spirit of depression, self-piety, jealousy, anger, hate, and envy. The adversary never lets you forget your past sins. He realizes that when you ask Jesus into your life and you accept Him as your personal Saviour, He blots out all your sins and remembers them no more. As a friend of mine would say, why "back yourself into enemy territory." Don't give him space to attack your peace. Put on the "helmet of salvation" which guards your mind. When a strong man fully guards his own house (mind), his mind is in peace. Whether you know it or not, an idle mind gives place to the adversary. Mediate on God's Word day and night. ***"But his delight is in the law of the Lord; and in his law doth he mediate day and night" (Psalms 1:2)***.

Rebuke the adversary when evil thoughts enter your mind. If you don't, you'll begin to act on the evil thoughts. Loving thoughts come from God and evil thoughts come from the adversary.

JOY

If you learn to have peace, then you can have joy. Joy is promised to the believers. No matter what trials or tribulations come your way, keep your joy. If the adversary

19

can capture your joy, then he has you. The joy of the Lord is your strength. No joy, no strength.

They that sow in tears shall reap in joy. ***"For weeping may endure for a night, but joy cometh in the morning" (Psalms 30:5)***. You might have to cry sometimes. But, that's all right; **Jesus** knows the meaning of every tear. He takes those tears, places them in a bottle, and knows the meaning of each tear.

As you go through the storms of life, keep your eyes on Jesus for He will sustain you. ***"Looking unto Jesus the author and finisher of our faith; who for the joy that was set before him endured the cross..." (Hebrews 12:2)***. Good examples are Paul and Silas, who were cast into prison for spreading God's Word. Yet, they kept their joy, and continued to sing songs of praise. Sometimes your finances may be touched, but keep rejoicing. Your health may be under attack, but keep rejoicing. Situations on your job may cause you to become oppressed, but keep rejoicing. Rejoice in the God of your salvation. (Habakkuk 3:18; Matthew 5:12; Luke 6:23).

Victory

After joy comes **VICTORY**. There is a song that says, "Don't wait until the battle is over; shout now." We have the **victory**. Aren't you glad? If you stand in the liberty and be not entangled with the yoke of bondage, you have victory.

We have victory over sin in our lives, if we are led by the Spirit. God will fight our battles. ***"Through God we shall do valiantly: for He it is that shall tread down our enemies" (Psalms 60:12)***. We are the head and not the tail; therefore, we have **power** to tread over evil.

Be determined that nothing shall separate you from the love of God. For everyone who is born of God overcomes the world. ***"For whatsoever is born of God overcometh the world: and this is the victory that overcometh the world, even our faith" (1 John 5:4)***.

REWARDS FOR OVERCOMERS

- Eat from the tree of life
- A new name
- Power
- Robe of righteousness
- A memorial pillar
- Sit with Me on My throne
- An inheritance

Witnessing

"Cry loud, spare not, lift up thy voice like a trumpet..."

Isaiah 58:1

CHAPTER 5

Who will be a **WITNESS** for the Lord? Who will, **"Cry loud, spare not, lift up thy voice like a trumpet..." (Isaiah 58:1)**. Are you willing to be used by God? We are living in an age where God's people are needed to go forth as never before.

As Born-Again Christians, we should say like Apostle Paul, **"For I am not ashamed of the gospel of Christ; for it is the power of God unto salvation to everyone that believeth..." (Romans 1:16)**. As believers in Christ Jesus we are to go about spreading the Good News. **"And the Lord said unto the servant, Go out into the highways and hedges,**

and compel them to come in, that my house may be filled" (Luke 14:23).

"For the Son of man is come to save that which was lost" (Matthew 18:11). God sent Jesus for a purpose, and we are here to carry out God's will. He went about doing the will of the Father without complaining. What about us?

Jesus was lied upon, hated, and rejected yet He never gave up. "...and ye shall be hated of all men for my name's sake." (Matthew 24:9) **"But he that shall endure unto the end, the same shall be saved" (Matthew 24:13)**.

Do not take your salvation for granted. Jesus prayed until sweat from His brow began to roll down as drops of blood. Then He said **"...O my Father, if it be possible, let this cup pass from me: nevertheless not as I will, but as thou wilt" (Matthew 26:39)**.

Today we must make a decision to let **God's** will be done in our lives. What is that will? The will is to be saved and filled with his Spirit and to come to know Him.

Some of you are saying, "I'm too young, I haven't begun to live," "there's a lot more in life that I want to do," and "wait until I get a little older." Psalms 85:8 says, **"Harden not your hearts, as in the** *provocation, and in the day of temptation..."*

Jesus is knocking at the door of your heart. All He wants you to do is open the door so He can come in. Let Jesus into your heart today. *"Behold I stand at the door, and knock: if any man hear my voice, and open the door, I will come in to him, and will sup with him, and he with me." (Revelation 3:20)*.

Jesus is the answer for the world today. There's no other name whereby man can be saved except by the name of Jesus. If they come any other way they're thieves and robbers, and the truth is not in them.

The Word tells us, *"That if thou shalt confess with thy mouth the Lord Jesus, and shalt believe in thine heart that God hath raised him from the dead, thou shalt be saved..." (Romans 10:9)*.

It is Jesus' wish that none should be lost. Although everyone will not be saved, it doesn't mean they can't be saved. Don't be the one who is lost. Take hold to Jesus today. Let Him become your Lord and Master.

What can wash away my sins? Only the Blood of Jesus. What can make me whole again? Only the Blood of Jesus. Truly, indeed, Jesus is a friend. He will never leave you nor forsake you; He will always walk by your side. At your weakest or lowest point, **"Look to the hills which cometh your help, because all your help cometh from the Lord who made heaven and earth" (Psalms 121:1-2)**.

The sheep in the fields have shepherds who lead and guide them. They direct them from the storms and wolves. Well, guess what? Jesus is our shepherd, and we shall not want. He knows what we need before we know, and He sees danger before we see it. That's why James tells us to **"Draw nigh to God, and he will draw nigh to you. Cleanse your hands, ye sinners; and purify your hearts, ye double minded" (James 4:8)**. Humble yourselves in the sight of the Lord, and He shall lift you up.

We draw nigh to God by surrendering our all to Him; we are sanctified by the Word of God. How can you hear without a preacher, and how can ye preach unless ye are sent?

When you give your life to Christ and accept His nature, continue to be steadfast and turn from evil to good. Don't just serve Him today and tomorrow do your own thing, and then, when trouble comes, run back to God. Be persistent. Be faithful to Him who is able to keep you from falling.

"A double minded man is unstable in all his ways" (James 1:8).

Overcoming Fear

"The Lord is my light and my salvation..."

Psalms 27:1

CHAPTER 6

We find today that many Saints of God are gripped by the four-letter word **"FEAR."** The only thing we have to fear is God. We are to serve the Lord with fear and rejoice with trembling. ***"Serve the Lord with fear, and rejoice with trembling" (Psalms 2:1)***. Let's discuss what fear is, what to do when it attacks, and the promises to those who fear God.

FEAR

First of all, FEAR is a spirit. Fear is a weapon that the adversary uses to hinder God's people. The adversary knows your fears and he knows if you are afraid, you will not accomplish the task that the Lord has laid upon you.

As Christians, we should not fear what man can do, but what God can do for He is able to kill the body and soul.

When we as Christians are walking with God and have submitted our lives totally to Him, we do not have to fear. *"...for greater is he that is in you, than he that is in the world" (1 John 4:4)*. When the adversary tries to overpower us with his spirit of fear (or any other spirits), remember to do the following:

- Go into the strongman's house and bind him;
- Rebuke the strongman in the Name of Jesus;
- Command the strongman to go back to the pit of Hell; and
- Begin to praise God for the overcoming victory.

This technique can be used whenever we are approached by any of the strongmen-spirit that presents itself if we know what spirit it is. Afterwards, respond to the situation as a soldier would when he has conquered a battle. For we are in a battle daily, but we are more than conquerors through Christ Jesus. Praise be to God!!! For He is worthy!!!

"I can do all things through Christ which strengtheneth me" (Philippians 4:13). On our own strength we can do nothing. We need to learn to depend on Jesus.

"...try the Spirit whether they are of God" (1 John 4:1). In order to be able to wrestle the **wiles** of the devil, we must know what the wiles are. We are not wrestling against flesh and blood. We are wrestling spirits. **Fear** is a spirit. We must be and should be able to recognize all spirits, before we can rebuke them.

One thing we must always remember is that God has not given us the Spirit of fear, but of power, and of love and of sound mind. Never fear anything. The Lord is always there to help us conquer any task. *"...The Lord is my helper, and I will not fear" (Hebrews 13:6)*.

If you have love you can conquer anything. *"There is no fear in love, but perfect love casteth out fear" (1 John 4:18).* The Lord promises us a sound mind, *"Thou wilt keep him in perfect peace, whose mind is stayed on thee" (Isaiah 26:3)*.

God wants us to serve Him. He only asks, that we fear Him, walk in His ways, and love Him with all our hearts and soul.

Advantages to those who FEAR God

Believe it or not there are some advantages to those who fear God. Listed below are just a few of them.

- His eye will be upon you
- His mercy
- Prolonged days
- Strong confidence and a place of refuge
- Instruction of wisdom
- Riches, honor, and life

Remember, God loves you and would do nothing to hurt you. Your enemy is Satan, for he comes to steal, kill, and destroy. Satan goes forth as a roaring lion, to and fro, seeking whom he may devour.

Steadfastness

"Therefore, my beloved brethren, be ye steadfast..."

1 Corinthians 15:58

CHAPTER 7

It is time for Christians to be persistent in their walk with the Lord. Today too many are giving up, falling down, and losing faith.

To be steadfast means to be firm in the belief, faithful, and determined. It is not enough to decide to follow Jesus; you must be determined. Can anyone question your walk, faithfulness, loyalty, love, or persistence in Christ?

We must be like a tree planted by the water, unmovable. When you plant a tree, the roots will begin to grow and take hold in the soil. Tree roots are wrapped so tight in the soil that it is hard to pull them up. As

Christians, we should be so rooted in **The Word of God** that nothing shall separate us from the love of Christ. ***"Who shall separate us from the love of Christ? Shall tribulations, or distress, or persecution, or famine, or nakedness, or peril or sword" (Romans 8:35)***.

Let us dwell, if you will, on the parable that speaks of two builders who built houses. One house was built on sand and the other built on a rock. Just think of yourself as a house built on sand. When the storms of life, criticisms, disappointments, circumstances, sicknesses, sorrows and griefs come your way, your house will not be able to stand because the house that is not built on a solid foundation cannot stand. The house will wash away.

Now imagine yourself as a house built upon a rock. When the storms of life, criticism, disappointments, circumstances, sickness, sorrow and griefs come, nothing can shake you because your foundation is sure. It is solid. You are determined to stand. As Edward Mote wrote, "My hope is built on nothing less than Jesus' blood and righteousness. I dare not trust the sweetest frame, but wholly lean on Jesus' name. On Christ, the solid rock I stand, all other ground is sinking sand."

Have you ever heard of a marathon? Guess what? We're running in a Christian marathon. Once we leave the starting line, we must continue until we finish. **"...he that endureth to the end shall be saved..." (Matthew 10:22)**. In this race, we cannot give up.

One thing we must remember as children of God is to never give up, be persistent, and strive for perfection. For your labour will not be in vain. **"...work while it is day for night cometh, when no man can work..." (John 9:4)**.

Learn to endure hardness as a good soldier. Paul told Timothy, a servant of the Lord, to endure. I am telling you today, "Endure." Whatever you go through is nothing compared to what Jesus went through.

When you find your faith weakening, ask for help. When Asa had to fight the battle against the enemy, King Baasha, God told Asa that He would be with him as long as he didn't forsake Him. He lets us know that He will never leave us nor forsake us. Just stay steadfast and don't forsake Him.

Whatever you do, never doubt. **"A double minded man is unstable in all his ways" (James 1:8)**.

There is so much work to be done. The good news of Jesus Christ must be spread.

When you look around and see the young and old being possessed with drugs, alcohol, prostitution, homosexuality, etc., it should cause your spirit to grieve. Jesus told his disciples to go into the highways and hedges and compel them to come.

What kind of picture are you painting for your brothers and sisters? Do they know that, *"The wages of sin is death, but the gift of God is eternal life" (Romans 6:23)*. They should. If not, you're not on your J-O-B.

We all have a job to do. That's why Jesus gave talents. If you do not know what your talents are, seek Him. Find out!

It's time to make a step. There are three steps.

- Pay your vows
- Make a commitment
- Surrender all

That's all. Remember the **vows** you made to God when you accepted Christ in your life. *"Better is it that thou shouldest not vow, than thou shouldest vow and not pay" (Ecclesiastes 5:5)*. Be **committed**. It seems we make commitments to this person or that person, but never to God. Most of all, surrender totally. Surrender all to Jesus. Give up all for the sake of Christ. ***"I count all things but loss for the excellency of the knowledge of Christ Jesus my Lord..." (Philippians 3:8)***.

So continue to praise the Lord no matter what comes your way. Sing victory songs. Refuse to be defeated.

Steadfastness

Prayer

"...thou shalt not be as the hypocrites are: for they pray...to be seen...but if you pray secretly, you will be rewarded openly."

Matthew 6:5-6

CHAPTER 8

What is prayer? Prayer is petitions offered to God for mercies desired and thanksgiving and praise for blessings received.

The first prayer mentioned was when Seth's son, Enos, was born. ***"...and he called his name Enos: then began men to call upon the name of the Lord..." (Genesis 4:26)***.

How many of you know that God does not hear you when iniquity is in your heart? (Psalms 66:18) Whether you are sinner or saint, when iniquity is in your heart your prayers will bounce like a ball off the wall. But if anyone be a worshiper of God, and do His will, God will hear him or her. When our prayers are not effective, we must go back to the altar and get it right with Him.

In Jesus' Sermon on the Mount, He said, "Blessed are the pure in heart; for they shall see God," therefore, we must be pure in order for Him to hear us. When malice, strife, jealousy, hatred, and envy abide, prayers are not answered. When husbands and wives are at odds with one another, prayers are hindered. With no forgiveness in your hearts, prayers are not heard.

Thank God for His Son, Jesus Christ. Christ paved the way for us. We can go into prayer in Jesus' name. So often we want to go to God with fancy words. But Christ left the Comforter (Holy Spirit) for us. We can have an advocate with the Father. Whereby we can cry Abba Father. ***"...for we know not what we should pray for as we ought: but the Spirit itself maketh intercession for us with groanings which cannot be uttered. And he that searcheth the hearts...because he maketh intercession for the saints according to the will of God" (Romans 8:26-27)***. He refers to Jesus Christ.

You find so many people start praying by using the word "Father". No, you cannot go directly to the Father. Jesus said that ***"I am the way, the truth, and the life: no man cometh unto the Father, but by me" (John 14:6).***

Prayer goes beyond falling down on your knees, or in whatever position you pray. There is inward and outward prayer. There are different postures in praying: kneeling, standing, bowing, or on your face before God.

Prayer can be administered anywhere. You don't necessarily have to be in church to pray. You may find yourselves praying to God in your cars, buses, work, home, malls, etc. I just want to warn you of some things that cause prayers to fail and what makes them successful.

Failures of Prayer

- Disobedience
- Doubting
- Iniquity
- Stubbornness
- Instability
- Selfishness

Successful in Prayer

- Humble
- Pure Heart
- Faith

- Confession
- Obedience

Take a few minutes to meditate on the above. Which category do you fall in? Praise Him!!

Praises be to God that He sent His Son, Jesus, to intercede on our behalf. We think we know what to pray for when we pray, but we don't. Thank God for Jesus because He makes intercession to the Father for us.

Those who have the Spirit, please do not forget to intercede for your brothers and sisters in the Lord. We are to bear the infirmities of the weak. Stop being concerned about your needs and pray for the needs of others. In doing this, you will be blessed by God.

Give Thanks

"O give thanks unto the Lord..."

Psalms 105:1

CHAPTER 9

The Lord deserves thanks for everything. For He made the Heavens and the Earth, etc. ***"In the beginning God created the heaven and the earth" (Genesis 1).*** He created man and woman. ***"So God created man in his own image, in the image of God created he him; male and female created him" (Genesis 1:27)***. Without God, we would be nothing.

We find that in the course of our lives, God has brought us out of many dangers. We were born in sin and shaped in iniquity. But He has brought me up also out of a horrible pit, out of the miry clay, and set my feet upon a rock, and established my goings. ***"But thanks be to God, which*** *giveth us the victory through our Lord Jesus Christ" (1 Corinthians 15:57)*.

In the midst of troubles we can call upon Him and He will answer. Just as He comes to our rescue in trouble, we can rescue others by telling them what God has done for us. *"God is our refuge and strength, a very present help in trouble"(Psalms 46:1)*.

We are not to be ashamed of the testimony of Jesus Christ. So often God brings us out of situations and we fail to even make known His deeds.

One reason God allows our trials and tribulations to come is so we might have a well of experience deep enough to draw from. With that experience we may have compassion and counsel to comfort our brothers and sisters.

We are to be thankful everyday. Many people celebrate the fourth Thursday of November as a day of giving thanks. The day of Thanksgiving should be everyday. For we are to be thankful everyday that God allows us to rise, lay down, breathe, walk, talk, and have our five senses. *"For in him we live, and move, and have our being..." (Acts 17:28)*. If anything, we should be able to share Thanksgiving Day with someone whose family is less fortunate, one who has no where to go, or with the sick or shut in.

I am reminded of the ten lepers. As they were walking along the roadside, Jesus came along and healed them. One of them, when he saw that he was healed, turned back and with a loud voice glorified God. The leper fell down on his face at Jesus' feet, giving Him thanks: the leper was a Samaritan. Of the ten lepers, only one came back to give thanks. This shows us how grateful he was.

Let's start giving thanks always for all things unto God the Father in the name of our Lord Jesus Christ.

Sing unto the Lord with songs of thanksgiving. Every time we enter into the house of God, we should be thankful. David said: ***"I was glad when they said unto me, Let us go into the house of the Lord" (Psalms 122:1)***. We should always be glad to assemble ourselves together in the house of the Lord.

I find today, you have to call people to see if they are coming or will come to church. With all the troubles that individuals are having, they should be running to the house of God.

In loving God, and knowing what He has brought us from and out of, there is joy in just thanking Him. We can never thank God enough. There is no amount of money great enough to pay Him for all He has done. All the praying, sacrificing, singing, giving, etc., unto Him will never do.

Thank God while you can. There may come a time when you cannot talk or wave your hands. Praise Him while you can. Give God the Glory in all things because He is worthy to be praised.

"Let your light so shine before men, that they may see your good works, and glorify your Father which is in heaven" (Matthew 5:16).

Let others see you praising and magnifying God and lifting up your head in the midst of your turmoil. *"But thou, Oh Lord, art a shield for me; my glory, and the lifter up of mine head" (Psalms 3:3)*.

Oh! Praise God!! For He is worthy!! Show to others that you can bless the Lord at all times, and His praises shall be continuously in your mouth.

Give thanks with a grateful heart. Give thanks to the Holy One because He is Jesus Christ our Lord.

Seek the Lord

"Draw nigh to God, and he will draw nigh to you..."

James 4:8

CHAPTER 10

Do you know what your call is? Do you know what your gift is? If not, why not? Have you been seeking and inquiring of the Lord? Or better still, do you want to know?

We are living in a day and time, when we should seek the Lord as never before. We need to know what it is He has for us to do.

As we look around, the work is before us. There is so much to do. The harvest is plentiful, but the laborers are few. Yes, there is work to be done in the vineyards, but where are the laborers? Where are the intercessors? Where are the witnesses? Where are the children of God?

So many are crying "Holy! Holy!" So many are professing Christ but not possessing. It is not enough to have Christ as your Saviour. He must be your Lord and Saviour. He must be the Lord of your life. He must always be in front and not in the back.

It is time to get real for the Lord. Time is out for slothfulness, wishy-washy saints, quiet and timid saints. The Lord is looking for bold soldiers. In order for a soldier to fight in the war, he must be strong and courageous. Uncle Sam can't use weak men in his army, and the Lord can't use weak and timid soldiers in His army.

Come on saints, let us rise and shine, for the glory of the Lord has risen. God has sent his Son Jesus to die for us. We are given a chance to be connected back to the Father. We were disconnected from the Father by the sin of Adam, and now God is giving us another chance to get it right.

Jesus said, "Why call me Lord, Lord and do not the things I say?" We all have a work to do. You have your own individual job to do for the Lord. He has given each of us a gift. Read the scripture on the Gifts. (Romans 12:6-8; 1 Corinthians 7:7) Which servant are you? Have you gained or have you lost out?

It is not the Lord's wish that we be lost or lack in the things He has us to do. In James 1:5-6 we read*, "If any of you lack wisdom, let him ask of God, that giveth to all men liberally, and upbraideth not; and it shall be given him. But let him ask in faith, nothing wavering..."* All we have to do is ask. We have not because we ask not.

Now there are diversities of gifts, but the same Spirit. And there are differences of administrations, but the same Lord. (1 Corinthians 12:4-5)

Manifestation of the Spirit

- Wisdom
- Word of knowledge
- Faith
- Gifts of healing
- Working of miracles
- Prophecy
- Discerning of spirits
- Divers kinds of tongues
- Interpretation of tongues

"But all these worketh that one and the selfsame Spirit, dividing to every man severally as he will" (1 Corinthians 12:8-11). What we must do is seek the Lord for our gift(s). Some have one and some have several.

The reason we enter the House of God is to come together for the edification of the Church. We come together on one accord that these gifts may be operating in the Church. The reason they are not operating is because someone has not sought the Lord to find out where their place is.

For the body is not one member, but many. The head cannot do without the neck; the neck cannot do without the shoulders; etc. We are one body. We function in unison.

Cammie B. Jeffress

The Love of God

For God so loved the world..."

John 3:16

CHAPTER 11

Jesus came to give life. God loved us so much that his Son gave his life. Even in all our disobedience, rebellion, and stiff-heartedness, God loved us so much that he sent His Son to give us His life that we may be connected back to Him. Through the sin of Adam, we were disconnected from the Father. Thank God for His mercy.

How many of us would give our life for our family, friend or stranger? None of us would go through what Jesus went through. Look around you today. So many are struggling within to follow Jesus, it should not be so. The way of the transgressor is hard.

Every year should be a year where the children of God come together on one accord. In order to make it to Heaven, we first have to get together here on Earth. Our love should be so genuine that when we see our fellow man down or struggling, we should have enough compassion to reach out and help him. As the Samaritan journeyed, he came across a young man wounded along side the road. What did he do? He had compassion for him. *"He went to him, and bound up his wounds, pouring in oil and wine, and set him on his own beast, and brought him to an inn, and took care of him" (Luke 10:33-34)*. The Samaritan acted out of love, and was not looking for anything in return.

We need to show love to this dying and sinful world. The reason the world is in such a turmoil is because of the lack of love. People are looking for love in all the wrong places and in the wrong things. It is our job to reinforce to them that Jesus is love.

Yes, my brothers and sisters we have a job to do. It is time to be doers of the Word of God. We must *"Go ye therefore, and teach all nations, baptizing them in the name of the Father, and of the Son, and of the Holy Ghost" (Matthew*

28:19). It is time to be about our Father's business.

There is a great work to be done. ***"We must work while it is day, for night cometh and no man can work" (John 9:4).*** Jesus said unto his disciples, ***"...The harvest truly is great, but the labourers are few: pray ye therefore the Lord of the harvest, that he would send forth labourers into his harvest" (Luke 10:2)***.

As children of God we are forever claiming to be born again, heaven bound, sanctified, wrapped up in Jesus, and love the Lord. Do you know that it is now time to confess all that you say?

It is time to go into the hedges and highway and compel dying men and women to come to Christ. Tell them that Jesus loves them; He is the way. He wants to help and deliver. Stop crying HOLY! Be ye holy as Christ is holy.

We all have a measure of love. If you do not know how to show or express the love that is within you, ask Jesus. ***"If you lack wisdom, let him ask of God, that giveth to all men liberally, and upbraideth not; and it shall be given him" (James 1:5)***. James refers to wisdom here as wisdom to understand God's Word.

We have not because we ask not. Whatever you need God has it. Just get your life in order and you can have it. There is always a condition to everything. Nothing is free. Jesus paid a terrible price for us. We could never repay him. All He asks once we have been set free, is for us to reach back and help our brothers and sisters. Jesus told Simon **"...But I have prayed for thee, that thy faith fail not: and when thou art converted, strengthen thy brethren" (Luke 22:31-32)**.

I just want to share this poem with you that the Lord led me to write in 1988:

LOVE

Love is giving,
Love is caring,
Love is essential,
Love is needed.

Love is kind,
Love is merciful,
Love is sweet,
Love is divine.

Jesus loves us,
This I know,
For the Bible,
Tells me so.

Jesus loves us,
More than we love ourselves,
In spite of our ways,
His love NEVER fails.

If you are not getting this type of love, you know it is not coming from a child of God. For charity [love] ***"Doth not behave itself unseemly, seeketh not her own, is not easily provoked, thinketh no evil..." (1Corinthians 13:5).***

The Love of God

Cammie B. Jeffress

The Power of God

"I am not ashamed of the gospel of Christ..."

Romans 1:16

CHAPTER 12

We are living in an era that needs God's Word as never before. Considering the events of this society today, as Christians, we are compelled to go forth in boldness and spread God's Word. There is no time for slothfulness, unconcerned individuals, or unfaithfulness to the ministry. God is calling for bold soldiers, those who do not mind standing for the Gospel's sake.

You've heard the old familiar song, "So many are falling by the wayside, Lord help me to stand." This song is so true today. Too many saints are taken down, giving up, being deceived, and can not stand to be rejected by the world today. They are forgetting that Jesus himself was hated. If the world hates you, **"And ye shall be hated of all men for my name's sake: but he that endureth to the end shall be saved" (Matthew 10:22).** Remember they hated Jesus before they hated you. So whether we are rejected, lied on, talked about, or laughed at, we must continue to spread the Word.

Just think for a moment if the Gospel was not spread to you, where would you be? So it is for those who are lost without knowledge of Christ. Once you have received Jesus Christ in your life and accepted His Holy Spirit, you are accountable to tell someone else. It is required of you, or the blood will be on your hands. Jesus told Simon Peter, **"...and when thy art converted, strengthen thy brethren" (Luke 22:32)**.

All the violence, drugs, abuses, etc., let us know that the Word of God is needed to be carried forth into the hedges and highways.

The days of comfort no longer exist. The children of God do not have time to sit back and relax. **"Awake out of sleep: for now is our salvation nearer than when we believed..." (Romans 13:11).**

The children of God are needed in the hospitals, nursing homes, prisons, streets, in front of the liquor stores, schools, bus and train stations, in general everywhere. I could go on and on. The key is are you doing it? Have you taken the time to give someone his or her dose of medication or hope for tomorrow?

Someone out there has lost sight of reality, lost knowledge of who they are, why they were born, and their purpose. First of all, you must know the answers for yourself before you can minister to anyone else.

Jesus said, *"...I was hungred and you gave me meat...I was sick, and ye visited me: I was in prison, and ye came unto me" (Matthew 25:35-36).* This is a verse that should be applied to you personally. If you can say yes to the above then thank God; you are sharing the Gospel.

So often, we, as children of God, spend so much time witnessing, praying and fasting for the saints that we do not have enough time to minister to the lost. Jesus said, *"They that be whole need not a physician, but they that are sick...I am not come to call the righteous, but sinners to repentance" (Matthew 9:12-13).*

Let us concentrate on spending more time and effort with the lost, for they are the ones in need of the physician. The feeble minded, hoary heads, sick, prisoners, alcoholics, drug addicts, prostitutes, etc., are the ones who need a physician. Jesus is able to heal the physical as well as the spiritual soul. He is concerned about the whole body: physically, spiritually, mentally, and financially.

Someone out there has lost sight of reality and hope, and does not know who they are, why they were born, and what their purpose is. Let me refresh your memory.

Who am I?

- Created by God
- Made in His image
- Fearfully and wonderfully made
- Complete in Him
- God fashioned us
- Peculiar people

Why was I born?

- For a purpose
- To serve God
- Eyes to read God's Word

- Body to represent God's temple
- Feet to walk in His ways
- Hands to do His will

What is our purpose in God?

- To glorify God and enjoy Him forever
- To become more like Jesus
- Reproduce that life in those whom you come in contact with to develop a Christ-like spirit
- Know the Word of God
- Witness of His goodness

Sing Unto the Lord

"O sing unto the Lord a new song..."

Psalms 98:1

CHAPTER 13

I will celebrate and sing unto the Lord. Let us sing to the Lord a new song. Give honor and glory to our Lord and Saviour Jesus Christ who is worthy of the highest praise.

It is good to be free to praise and magnify the Lord. The praises of the Lord are so important to God's people. When you are free and go forth in the praises, anyone around you who is bound can be set free. ***"Now the Lord is that Spirit: and where the spirit of the Lord is, there is liberty" (2 Corinthians 3:17)***. In freedom, the spirit can move from heart to heart and breast to breast, causing any sinners to be touched, or saint to be loosed by the Holy Spirit.

Sing unto God, no matter what situation you are facing or confronted with. The devil cannot stand God's children to praise God because the adversary knows he must flee. *"O praise the lord, all ye nations, praise him all ye people for his merciful kindness is great towards us" (Psalms 117:1-2).*

Bless the Lord at all times, let His praise be forever in your mouths. Let your request be known unto God. Let Him know how much you love and adore him. Give Him thanks for all He has done in your lives, for your family, your spiritual growth, your physical health, your financial situations, etc.

There are moments in your life when you go through low periods and may not be able to go forth in praises as you should. Do not fret when this happens. Praise Him regardless. For we as children of God, go through these times. Nevertheless, continue to rejoice in the Lord. Keep on singing for the joy of the Lord is your strength. No joy, no strength.

Sometimes we are troubled on every side, yet not distressed; we are perplexed, but not in despair. *"Persecuted, but not forsaken; cast down, but not*

destroyed..." (2 Corinthians 4:8-9).
That is why the **Word of God** tells us to
***"Put on the whole armour of God, that
we may be able to stand against the
wiles of the devil" (Ephesians 6:11).***
Never take your armor off. Always keep the
armor on so that the fiery darts of the devil
will not be able to penetrate. "Put on the
whole armour of God, that ye may be able
to stand against the wiles of the devil"
(Ephesians 6:10).

Why do we keep this armor on? We
keep it on, ***"For we wrestle not against
flesh and blood, but against
principalities, against powers, against
the rules of the darkness of this world,
against spiritual wickedness in high
places" (Ephesians 6:12).***

What does all that mean? It means you
are not fighting against your brothers or
your sisters, but against the devil and his
little foes that are set out to attack you.
The devil does not care about you or
anyone else. His main purpose is to **stop
the children of God from lifting up the
name of Jesus, singing God's praises,
and spreading the Word**.

Let us be wise, as the spirit-filled
children of God should be. Keep in mind the
five wise virgins who kept oil (Holy Spirit)
in their vessels and were ready when the

bridegroom came. So keep your vessel with oil that you may be able to stay in the spirit realm to see and recognize the attacks and not the carnal realm where darkness prevents you from seeing. To be carnal-minded is death, but spiritual-minded is life.

Those who are not familiar with this scripture may say, what is the armor. This is the armor:

- Loins girt with truth
- Having on the breastplate of righteousness
- Feet shod with the preparation of the gospel of peace
- Taking the shield of faith
- Helmet of salvation
- Sword of the spirit, which is the Word of God

After all the armor is on: ***"Praying always with all prayer and supplication in the Spirit..." (Ephesians 6:14-18).***

Thy Word

"Thy word is a lamp unto my feet, and a light unto my path."

Psalms 119:105

CHAPTER 14

The Word of God is much needed today.

Have you ever planned a trip and did not know the direction to take? Have you ever relied on AAA or some other travel club to map the way for you? Well, if you have confidence in the travel agencies to get you from one destination to another, why not have confidence in the Word of God to get you out of sin and on your way to eternal life?

"Thy word have I hid in my heart, that I might not sin against thee" (Psalms 119:11). We are living in the last days, and destruction is all around us, but

God is our refuge and strength, a very present help in time of trouble.

So many today are feasting off the carnal things of this world and not the Word of God. In Psalms 119, God's Word promises us so much. Listed below are just a few descriptions of what God's Word is:

- Cleansing
- Counseling
- Strength
- Hope
- Salvation
- Understanding

When Jesus was led up in the spirit into the wilderness to be tempted by the devil, and fasted forty days and forty nights, it was the Word of God that put the devil to flight. And today, it is going to take the Word of God, because the devil only flees when the Word is spoken.

The Word is a powerful source. ***"For the word of God is quick, and powerful, and sharper than any twoedged sword, piercing even to the dividing asunder of soul and spirit, and of the joints and marrow, and is a discerner of the thoughts and intents of the heart"*** *(Hebrews 4:12)*.

Through the Word we gain faith. ***"For faith cometh by hearing and hearing by the word of God" (Romans 10:17)***. How can we gain faith without reading and believing God's Word? Faith is believing God's Word whether you see it or not. If you do not know God's Word, how can you believe God's Word?

In the Scriptures are the proclamations of great divine promises of God, which are made available to us in His Word. Most of us, today, do not take the time to find out what is available to us in our times of adversities. Remember and hide these basic scriptures in your heart:

- **Cast-down head:**

    But thou, O Lord, art a shield for me; my glory, and lifter up of mine head. (Psalms 3:3)

- **Fearful:**

    Yea, though I walk through the valley of the shadow of death, I will fear no evil: for thou art with me; thy rod and thy staff they comfort me. (Psalm 23:4)

- **Trust:**

  Trust in the Lord with all thine heart, and lean not unto thy own understanding. In all thine ways acknowledge Him, and He shall direct thy path. (Proverbs 3:5-6)

- **Whatever situation:**

  I will bless the Lord at all times: his praise shall continually be in my mouth. (Psalm 34:1)

- **Mercy:**

  Have mercy upon me, O God, according to thy loving-kindness: according unto the multitude of thy tender mercies blot out my transgressions. (Psalm 51:1)

- **Forgiveness:**

  But if ye do not forgive, neither will your Father which is in heaven forgive your trespasses. (Mark 11:26)

- **Help**

    I will lift up mine eyes unto the hills, from whence cometh my help. My help cometh from the Lord, which made heaven and earth.(Psalm 121:1-2)

- **Confession:**

    If we confess our sins, he is faithful and just to forgive us our sins, and to cleanse us from all unrighteousness. (1 John 1:9)

- **Peace:**

    Peace I leave with you, my peace I give unto you; not as the world giveth, give I unto you. Let not your heart be troubled, neither let it be afraid. (John 14:27)

- **Assurance:**

    He that dwelleth in the secret place of the most High shall abide under the shadow of the Almighty. (Psalms 91:1)

- **Forsaken:**

    I have been young, and now am old; yet have I not seen the righteous forsaken, nor his seed begging bread. (Psalm 37:25)

- **Evil Spirits:**

    Beloved, believe not every spirit, but try the spirits whether they are of God: because many false prophets are gone out into the world. (1 John 4:1)

Take time to study and research and meditate on the **Word of God** until you get a clear understanding.

Let us be first partakers of the fruits (Word). ***"The husbandman that laboureth must be first partaker of the fruits" (2 Timothy 2:6).*** In order to be a partaker of the Word, you must first apply the Word to your life. Christians today are, ***"Ever learning, and never able to come to the knowledge of the truth" (2 Timothy 3:7).*** Why? Because they are always applying the Word to others.

We must learn to be doers of the Word, and not just hearers only. By being just a hearer you deceive your own self. ***"For if***

any be a hearer of the word, and not a doer, he is like unto a man beholding his natural face in a glass..." (James 1:23-24).

Defeat the Giants

"...greater is he that is in you..."

1 John 4:4

CHAPTER 15

Do you have Giants in your life? Do you know what a Giant is or can be? A Giant can be anything that you allow to defeat you from doing God's will. A Giant is not always a person, it can be situations, trials, or even spirits that prevent you from going forth as God directs.

David had to fight the Giant, and you today have to do the same thing in order to be free. ***"Ye are of God, little children, and have overcome them: because greater is he that is in you, than he that is in the world" (1 John 4:4)***.

You cannot sit back and allow the Giants to overcome you, walk on you, and defeat you. Whatever you do, do not allow it to bring fear. You have been given the power;

use it. If you are walking upright, operating in the will of God, in fellowship with Him, and being obedient to His will, you have that right. But if you lack any of the above, watch out for you are doomed.

There are three enemies that can hinder you: the adversary, flesh, and self. Which one will you allow to rob you of the privileges of being God's child? ***"Ye did run well; who did hinder you that ye should not obey the truth" (Galatians 5:7).*** Guess who? YOU!!!! Because our worst enemy is ourselves.

You must realize that there are two wills. The **perfect will** and the **submissive will**. The perfect will is when you are operating and being directed by the Holy Spirit in total obedience. The submissive will is when you decide to disobey the Holy Spirit and do things the way your mind directs. When we are disobedient to God, we run into so many snares, traps, complications, and disappointments. In following the path that has been mapped for us, you will find rest, comfort, joy, peace, and contentment.

When we go contrary to the Will of God, we give place to the adversary. Therefore, we allow ourselves to be backed up on the adversary's territory. The adversary was put in his place when Jesus took the keys of death, Hell, and the grave. Not only that, but Jesus put the adversary under His feet, where the adversary belongs. Keep the adversary under you feet. Take control over the giants in your life. *"Stand fast therefore in the liberty wherewith Christ hath made you free, and be not entangled again with the yoke of bondage" (Galatians 5:1).*

Your giants are not just people, for you are in spiritual warfare. *"For the weapons of our warfare are not carnal, but mighty through God to the pulling down of strong holds" (2 Corinthians 10:4)*.

David's giant was a 9-foot 9-inch giant named Goliath. (1 Samuel 17:4) The giant threatened the Philistines by asking *"...give me a man, that we might fight together" (1 Samuel 17:10)*.

You know the story. David approached the giant with a few smooth stones and a sling, the stone sunk into the giant's forehead, and he fell with his face to the ground. That was the Lord. The giant fell dead. David knew that the battle was not his, but the Lord's.

As Christians today, we must also know as David knew, that the battles in our lives are not ours, they belong to the Lord. The Lord is our rock, and fortress, and deliverer.

Those of you facing giants today, take a stand. Stand up and be counted as a child of God. Refuse to let the tricks and deceit of the adversary overtake you in your battles. Our weapon is the Word of God. Speak it boldly.

Go to the enemy camp and take back what belongs to you. You have the right to demand whatever you have lost to be restored. Do not be robbed of your:

- Joy
- Faith
- Praise
- Love
- The Word

Everything that has been taken from you, **"TAKE IT BACK."**

As you walk through those valleys, fear no evil. Why? Because surely, goodness and mercy shall follow you and peace is before you.

CONQUER THE LAND!!!

DEVOUR THE ENEMY!!!

RECLAIM WHAT IS YOURS!!!

REFERENCES

The New Analytical Bible and Dictionary of the Bible Authorized King James Version Comprehensive General Index Edition. (1973). Iowa Falls, Iowa: John A, Dickson Publishing Company.

Life Application Bible: New King James Version. (1993). Wheaton, Illinois: Tyndale House Publishers, Inc.

Ogilvie, Lloyd John. (1982) *Nelson's Three-in-One Bible Reference Companion*. Nashville: Thomas Nelson Publishers.

Willmington, H.L. (1987). *Willmington's Book of Bible Lists*. Wheaton, Illinois: Tyndale House Publishers, Inc.

ABOUT THE AUTHOR

Elder Dr. Cammie B. Jeffress is a native of Alexandria, Virginia. She is affiliated with the Saint Paul Christian Center, Alexandria, Virginia.

Dr. Jeffress accepted the Lord Jesus Christ as her Lord and Saviour on November 11, 1974, at Saint Paul Pentecostal Church, Inc., under the leadership of her Aunt, the Late Overseer Harriette E. Wood. She was called into the Ministry in September 1981 and later called by the Lord to Pastor in December 1991, where she became the Founder and Pastor of the Praise and Deliverance Ministries, Dumfries, Virginia.

Later, the Lord led her to establish a Bible Institute. Dr. Jeffress established the Praise and Deliverance Bible Institute from September 1993 to April 1996. She is an affiliated member and an Advance Teacher of the Evangelical Training Association (ETA/CEU), Advanced High Standards of Church Ministries Program, Wheaton, Illinois. In April 1997, the name of the Institute was changed to the H. E. Wood Bible Institute, which became a separate entity and received its World Wide

Accreditation from the Commission of Christian Educational Institutions in Richmond, Virginia.

Dr. Jeffress has been received in to the International Who's Who of Entrepreneurs. She is a Commonwealth of Virginia Notary Public, Appointee by His Excellency the Governor, State of Virginia.

Dr. Jeffress graduated from the Spirit of Truth Institute with a Doctorate of Church Administration, and an Honorary Doctorate in Christian Education.

Scriptures

Worship — to honor or reverence

Worshipping God

-Col. 4:16; 1 Timothy 4:13	reading God's word
-Acts 6:2, 2 Timothy 2:15	studing God's word
-1 Corinthians 11:2	keeping of the ordinances
-Acts 2:41; 3:1; 4:31	lifting up of prayers, intercessions
-Ephesians 6:18	supplications and thanksgiving
-Hebrews 13:15	sacrifice of our praise
-Hebrews 13:16	sacrifice of our good works
-Philippians 4:18	sacrifice of our substance

<u>Praise</u> — to express; to glorify God

<u>Times of Praise</u>:

-Psalms 72:15	daily
-Psalms 71:6	continually
-Psalms 119:164	seven times daily
-Psalms 35:28	all the day
-Psalms 119:62; Acts 16:25	at midnight
-Psalms 146:2	while I live
-Psalms 43.3	with my lips

<u>Fear</u> — anxiety caused by approaching danger

<u>Causes of</u> :

-Genesis 3:10   disobedience
-John 20.19   persecution
-Acts 9:26   suspicion
-2 Corinthians 11:3   uncertainty
-Hebrews 2:15   death

<u>Effects of</u>:

-1 Samuel 13:5-8   demoralization
-Mathew 28.4   paralysis
-John 9:22   silent testimony

Prayer — a petition to God; an earnest request

<u>For deliverance</u>:

-Jacob's prayer	Genesis 32:9-12
-David's prayer	Psalms 31, 57, 142
-Disciples prayer	Matthews 8:24-25
-Peter's prayer	Matthews 14:28-31

<u>For forgiveness</u>:

-2 Samuel 24:10	number of the people
-Psalms 32, 51	for immorality
-Job 40:3-4; 42:6	for pride
-Luke 15:17-19	backsliding

Steadfastness — firmness, persistence, and
determination in one's endeavors

> Spiritual things:
>
> -Hebrews 12:7   enduring chastisement
> -Romans 35:1-19   bearing persecution
> -Hebrews 3,6,14   perserverence
> -Colossians 2:5   stability in faith
> -Galatians 5:1   defending Christian
>   liberty

<u>Love</u> — unselfish, benevolent concern for others, brotherly concern

Love that a Christian is to exhibit:

<u>Toward God</u>:

-Matthew 22:37-38	First Commandments
-Matthew 22:37	With all the heart

<u>Toward Christ</u>:

-John 8:42	Signs of true faith
-John 14:15, 21, 23	Manifestations of obedience
-2 Corinthians 5:14	Leads to service

<u>Victory</u> — winning the mastery in battle over odds or difficulties

<u>Victory over</u>:

-Galatains 6:16-21   Flesh
-1 John 5:4   World
-James 4:7   Satan

<u>For Christians</u>:

-Philippians 4:13   Through Christ
-Galatians 6:16, 17, 22, 25   Holy Spirit

<u>Overcome</u> — to conquer

   <u>By</u>:

-2 Peter 2:19, 20	Fleshly desires
-Romans 8:37	God

   <u>Objects</u>:

-John 16:33	World
-Romans 12:21	Evil
-1 John 4:4	Evil spirits
-Revelations 17:13-14	Evil powers